CHARITY

The Gifts of Giving

*Discover the hidden benefits of
kindness and generosity*

GARRET BISS

*GARRET
B
2017*

TABLE OF CONTENTS

INTRODUCTION

REQUESTS FOR CHARITABLE donations surround us. They bombard us on the radio and television. They pop up on the computer and ring through our phones. We find solicitations plastered around checkout counters and filling our mailboxes. Occasionally, you may even have someone knock on your door looking for a contribution to his or her cause.

Charity is a big part of our culture. You see it through the organization and support of soup kitchens and through volunteer efforts within the community. Many world religions advocate regular contribution to charity. In fact, tithing, giving 10 percent of your income, is a regular practice in most religions.

Nearly everyone would agree that donating to charity is a good thing, but few people actually make charitable involvement a normal part of their lives. We talk about the benefits of exercise or eating a balanced diet, and know these are good things to do. But we routinely fail to take the appropriate actions so we miss out on the benefits. The same is true about giving to charity.

Through my own involvement in charitable giving, I have come to understand and see the benefits of my involvement, what I refer to as "The Gifts of Giving". I have found through my own experience, and by speaking to others, that donors often receive substantial benefits from the act of giving either time or resources.

Giving is certainly a noble and righteous act, but we are not necessarily inspired to do it for that reason alone. This book's purpose is to educate readers about the many benefits that come with charitable efforts – beyond the obvious benefit provided to the recipient. Like the reminder about proper nutrition and exercise for physical health, this book is a lesson in how acts of charity can provide you spiritual health by bringing joy, happiness and vitality to your life.

> *"The only care*
> *That I shall share*
> *Shall be the care of others,*
> *And on the road*
> *I'll halve the load*
> *Of overburdened brothers.*

I rather guess
    It's selfishness
    That drives me to such actions,
    For in this plan
    I find I can
    Forget my own distractions."

–John Kendrick Bangs

Whether for selfishness or righteousness, everybody wins when someone gives.

CHAPTER ONE
The Gifts of Giving

"When I do good, I feel good; when I do bad,
I feel bad; and that's my religion."
–Abraham Lincoln

CHARITY HAS BECOME a very important part of my life in recent years. Through my acts of service, I have had the wonderful fortune to understand and experience many benefits that come from performing a selfless act to help others. Often, the greatest benefactor is the person or group receiving the gift, and rightly so. But I have come to know and enjoy many of the benefits that an act of charity can provide to the person making the contribution. This recent experience, and the personal reflections I have had on the Gifts of Giving, inspired me to write this book so that I may share these ideas for the benefit of others.

I believe there are many great causes in the world that are in need of charitable support. Any act of charity is a noble act in itself. It is easy to comprehend the benefits of charity at face value. Everyone understands that every meal provided to a starving child, each terminal illness prevented, homeless person sheltered or life improved through charity is a great thing. No one would argue that less charity would make the world better. Yet, somehow, many of us do not make as significant a donation to charity as we could, if we make one at all. I believe in the notion that if someone harms another, all are harmed. Similarly, if someone helps another, everyone is helped. We are all in this together.

If we could each appreciate the many gifts of charity that lay beyond the act itself, we might be inspired to give of ourselves with a greater regularity and abundance. The more each of us gives of our time, energy or resources for the benefit of others, the better we will all enjoy this life. If this book inspires just one person to make a contribution to charity that he or she otherwise would not have made, the goal of this book will have been achieved. I truly believe that everyone benefits when somebody gives.

CHAPTER TWO
What is Charity?

"Do what you can, with what you have,
where you are."
–Theodore Roosevelt

THE IDEA OF charity means different things to different people. Some consider charity to be giving money to a specific cause. Others consider serving in a soup kitchen or building a home for someone in need to be the definition of charity.

Merriam-Webster defines charity[1] as: "(noun) The act of giving money, food, or other kinds of help to people who are poor, sick, etc." This is likely the most common understanding of what charity is – a contribution of a material possession

1. http://www.merriam-webster.com/dictionary/charity, accessed 22 July, 2014.

given to another who is in need.

Webster's definition continues, "Benevolent goodwill toward or love of humanity; Generosity and helpfulness especially toward the needy or suffering; also: aid given to those in need." This definition suggests that charity can be more than a material gift; it can also include a feeling of goodwill or generosity toward others.

I understand the concept of charity to extend far beyond the common idea of providing a gift to the needy. I believe charity goes on to mean every gift of time, thought, energy or material good donated to someone in need. This can mean a gift to a starving child or homeless family, or a gift to a friend, whether that friend is needy or not.

I believe charity encompasses the range of activities done for the benefit of another. It can be a financial donation for a well in Africa or a kind act done for a friend facing a rough patch. This book will show how any act or donation of charity, regardless of the recipient's circumstances, will produce benefits from the same Gifts of Giving.

Every definition of charity refers to the act of thinking about the benefit of another before your own. When you commit an act of charity, whether it is a kind gesture or a donation for a worthy cause, you are completing that act with another in mind. This is the point that allows all the other magic of charity to happen. It is the moment when you put another's needs before your own, an act that is not just a noble concept. Your brain actually changes when you reach beyond yourself to give. Giving is not just beneficial for the recipient; in so many ways, it is good for the person making the donation.

» ACTION

FOR THE NEXT 3 DAYS, write down all of your charitable acts – any act of kindness or donation to charity you make. Also, recall and write down your past charitable acts and remember how they made you feel. During these 3 days, make the most of this activity. Stretch from your comfort zone and go out of your way to do something for another.

CHAPTER THREE
Positive Energy

"Life engenders life. Energy creates energy. It is by
spending oneself that one becomes rich."
–Sarah Bernhardt

GIVING HELPS THE charitable person because the act itself creates positive energy. One important point to understand is that in this world there is both positive and negative energy. This may be harder to understand in the context of physical things (the concept of anti-matter, for example, is hard for most people to grasp), but for emotions, it is quite easy.

Every emotion we experience is either positive or negative in nature. Hatred, envy, frustration, guilt and a long list of other emotions can all be categorized as negative energy emotions. On the other side of the emotional spectrum, you have everything that is positive in nature - love, happiness, gratitude, appreciation, joy, etc.

As people, we have the ability to create emotional energy. Positive emotions, derived from positive energy, can inspire us to commit positive acts. The positive acts we commit have the ability to create positive emotions in our heart. The act of opening a door for another person is a positive act; one which will create a positive emotion of appreciation in another person.

Enjoying an emotion of gratitude or joyfulness often inspires us to commit positive acts, like complimenting a stranger or leaving a big tip for your server. I don't wish to belabor a discussion on the alternative, but it is important to see that the opposite is also true. Negative energy emotions inspire negative acts like rude behavior, yelling and violence. Each of these acts has the potential to manifest negative emotions in those who experience the act.

Neuroscience explains this phenomenon. Our thoughts and feelings are tied to actions. Even when we hear people use words that describe actions, the motor areas of the brain are activated as if we were actually doing the action described. Our brains are organized so that ideas and actions are intimately connected, as you will learn later when you read about research in cognitive science. Our feelings inspire actions, and our actions inspire feelings.

Understanding positive and negative energy emotions can empower you to leverage your own actions and emotions. When you commit an act that inspires a positive emotion, that act creates a positive emotion in you and in the person who benefits from the act. By presenting a friend with a nice gift, you feel a positive emotion inside. You may experience the warmth of love or the happiness for your friendship. When your friend receives the gift, he or she will likely feel gratitude and appreciation. One act committed creates a positive emotion for both of you. But it doesn't stop there.

Positive emotions can inspire positive actions. With your good feeling, you may share your positive energy with others when you are inspired to compliment or lend a hand to a stranger. Your friends may also commit similar acts that are inspired by the positive emotions they now embrace. Your one gift has created a wave of positive energy that can spread far beyond you or your friend.

The greatest benefit of positive energy is what it does to negative energy and negative emotions. If you were having a bad day and experiencing many negative emotions, how would you react if someone gave you a thoughtful and generous gift?

Imagine you recently came home from a very stressful day at work. Maybe all you could think about was the stress of work piling up on your desk, the lack of appreciation you felt from your boss, or the rude behavior of a few co-workers. You may understandably feel some negative emotions like frustration, anxiety, anger and maybe even hatred.

Now, imagine later that evening a very close friend of yours stopped by to give you a wonderful gift; maybe it was a gift certificate to your favorite restaurant or a small trinket that you really enjoyed. Imagining how you would feel, what changed in the emotions you held? Did the severity of your anger and frustration diminish, if only for a moment? Did the hatred you experienced earlier begin to fade?

One way to think of the relationship between positive and negative emotions is to equate them to hot and cold water. Let's pretend that negative energy is akin to cold water and positive emotional energy is like hot water. When you feel the negative emotions of cold water, if someone were to share some warm water with you, it would warm up your negative emotions. The amount of temperature increase would be relative to the amount and temperature of the cold water in your cup. A little hot water for a short time would warm your negative emotions just a little. A sustained flow of hot water for a long enough period would help you reverse the coldness of your water and bring you back to warm, positive emotions.

Charity can be an effective way to increase the positive energy in your emotions. When we give of ourselves selflessly to benefit another, this act creates a very warm and positive emotional response in our heart and mind. The greater the contribution, the greater the positive feeling we receive from the act. The more continuously we donate to charity, the more warmth we continue to feel. This positive and warm feeling we enjoy can be a wonderful benefit of charity.

The human brain is wired for social connection, bonding and giving. Oxytocin, the so-called "love hormone," is secreted during bonding and connection. It's probably part of the reason that giving of ourselves literally feels good. There is also a healing component to this. Many people believe that giving is good for our health. The hormone oxytocin is actually associated with a reduction in inflammation, the basis of many ailments and symptoms. There is, therefore, a real connection between giving in its broadest sense and well-being.

It won't surprise you to learn that in addition to the release of oxytocin, giving is associated with a reduction in the stress response. When giving, the brain literally experiences a flow of positive energy that can neutralize the anxiety inherent in the fight-flight reaction. Giving results in measurable and real changes in brain chemistry. In short, giving of yourself is a great stress management tool.

I have used this gift of charity many times in my life. There have been days when I faced minor struggles or felt negative emotions clouding my mind. When this happens, I will often turn my attention to charity and commit an act of giving for the benefit of another. Sometimes, this act is a quick donation to one of the charities I support. Other times, I will stop to grab a small gift for a friend. Either way, this short diversion from my own problems and the positive energy I create through my act are usually enough to erase the negative emotions or concern I felt and get me back to feelings of appreciation or gratitude.

At one time in my life, I was experiencing a very difficult and dark period. I faced career and personal challenges that cast a shadow over my life and emotional state. I effectively used a habit of daily charitable contributions to help me get through that period. The positive energy and emotions I received from these small but regular acts of charity certainly didn't erase the challenge I was facing in my life. It did, however, provide some positive energy and regular moments of reprieve from my stress. I found this made a huge difference.

The challenge is something I still face, but my contribution and focus on charity during this time has made this period in my life bearable. Reducing stress and depression is a gift we enjoy from charity.

» ACTION

THE NEXT TIME you find yourself stressed or experiencing a negative emotion, take a moment to make a small donation to charity or commit an act of kindness towards another. Reflect on this experience and the effect it had on your emotions and the stress you felt.

CHAPTER FOUR
A Sense of Control

"I have found that among its other benefits, giving
liberates the soul of the giver."
–Maya Angelou

W HEN WE FEEL overloaded with pressure or preoccupation of mind, we often limit the flow of positive energy that normally emanates from us. We "go internal" and focus our time and energy on thoughts and mental preparation. We guard our mind from distraction by focusing our attention inward or on the task at hand. If you have ever been around people like this, they may seem cut off, fidgety, or easily agitated.

There is a Universal principle referred to as the Law of Cause and Effect. In philosophic terms, this law simply suggests that the energy you put out into the Universe is the energy you get back. Think of it as good or bad karma. What would this law suggest about the act of "going internal" or becoming preoccupied with personal concerns?

When we stop putting our normal positive energy out into the environment around us, how does that affect the way the Universe responds to us? What do you attract from the environment around you when you are putting out negative energy? At a time when we need a surplus of goodwill from the Universe, we may actually be taking actions that create a greater deficit.

Throughout life we all face stressful times. An upcoming project at work, an exam in school or a major life change like making a move or buying a house can all add to the stress of our life. Many of the events and challenges we face in life take their toll on our attention, mood and energy; depleting our ability to focus on other things. Sometimes, the stress from challenges we face will last beyond the point we can do anything about it.

The next time you have such an event looming over you, try to take the opposite approach. Take purposeful actions to create a debt of positive energy from the Universe. Spend the energy you have being extra kind to others, buy something small for someone at work, or give some money to charity. Give a friend a compliment or help someone with a project he or she is working on. Then, watch and see if that positive energy finds its way back to you.

A few months ago, I completed a course for a real estate brokerage license. The course was given over a 9-week period. A little more than half way into the course, we took a midterm exam. I had spent much of the previous five weeks preparing for this exam and had devoted nearly every available minute of the last five days to studying my notes. The exam was scheduled for one evening immediately after work, so when I went to bed the night before, I had done all the preparation I would have the time to do.

On the day of the exam, I had little on my mind besides the test I would soon take. Meetings and projects at work robbed me of any opportunity to flip through my notes one last time, but the pending test was still all I had on my mind. I knew there was nothing more I could do to prepare, but I worried that I hadn't done enough. I was certain there was something I forgot to study that would show up and bite me on the exam.

I felt stressed most of the day, and this stress took its toll on my attention for my job and on my mood. My time for studying had come and gone, but the worry remained, and it affected everything else I was doing. I survived the midterm that evening, but I realized the cost on my emotional energy and productivity was a price I shouldn't have to pay.

If you think back to our discussion on energy, you can see how allowing these negative emotions to fester in my mind that day was the worst thing I could have done. Stress and anxiety perpetuated negative energy into the environment around me, and that drew other negative feelings to my attention. When the evening arrived and I finally sat to take the exam, much of my physical energy had been drained by the anxiety I felt all day. An anxious state of mind, with a negative emotional energy, is the worst mood to carry into the testing room. This negative emotional energy can stifle focus and the ability to remember what you studied. The negative energy of stress attracts other negative emotions like doubt or insecurity, not something you want when trying to recall information during an exam.

The result: I scored a 78% on the exam; 80% was considered passing.

A few weeks later, I faced a similar situation with my final exam. This time I was intent on finding a way to distract my mind from the test anxiety I would soon face. Knowing that we create positive energy from charity, I decided to use charity to protect my emotional energy and replace the negative anxiety and stress I would otherwise face. I took control.

The day of the final exam, I began the morning by purchasing coffee for a few coworkers on my way to work. This gesture, and my coworkers' positive response, helped to displace some of the test anxiety I was facing. After getting some work done, I stopped for a moment to write emails to a few friends and coworkers. I took this opportunity to either share something I appreciated about them or to thank them for something they had recently done. The time I spent thinking of others and completing another kind, selfless gesture was a distraction for the stress I would have experienced by worrying about my final.

Before I left work for the day and drove to the testing center, I pulled up a website on the computer and donated to a charity I like to support. This act of generosity and charity filled me with a positive energy once again and stimulated many positive emotions in my mind. The donation created feelings of gratitude for what I had and was able to share with others. I felt great for doing something to help others in need.

These positive thoughts and emotions replaced the anxiety and uncertainty I would have otherwise carried into the testing center. You would have to experience it to believe it, but the emotions of stress and doubt I had during the midterm were replaced by confidence and ease of mind. The result of my confidence and low stress was a grade of 95 percent. I aced it!

I am reminded of a study conducted by John Bargh and his colleagues at New York University in which student volunteers were asked to create phrases from different sets of five words. One set of five words was "Florida, forgetful, bald, grey, wrinkle." The variable that was being measured was the time taken to walk down the corridor to an assigned room after subjects had completed the task.

Subjects who had been thinking about words associated with old age walked down the corridor significantly slower than those who saw lists of words that had nothing to do with aging. When shown the results, the subjects were very surprised as they had no conscious awareness of the impact of their previous activity on their speed of movement. This research, and other projects like it, demonstrate that what we are mentally processing does affect us, even when we are unaware of it. The "Florida effect" shows that not only do words have associations, but those associations are also reflected in bodily movements, as well as thoughts and ideas in our head.

This is just one example of how acts of charity can help us take control of our emotions and, ultimately, the outcome of our life experiences. The next time you face an important event with work or in life, use acts of charity to take control of your emotions and improve your outcome. Help stimulate your own positive energy by completing selfless acts of generosity for the benefits of others. Positive energy will manifest as feelings of confidence and enthusiasm with others.

Use this technique for any major event you face; it could be just as effectively used to improve your performance during the next major sales pitch, big presentation, or important speech. Acts of charity will improve the way you interact with others and the results you experience in life.

» ACTION

Before tackling your next challenging task, take a moment and commit an act of generosity or make a charitable donation to your favorite cause.

CHAPTER FIVE
Change Your Perspective

*"You must look within for value but
must look beyond for perspective."*
–Denis Waitley

A COMMON YET UNFORTUNATE reality of life is that we all encounter times of challenge or disappointment. We face difficult events in our life and live with the consequences of days past. Stress, frustration and anxiety tend to be a normal part of this life experience. Some periods of misfortune and stress act like black rain clouds that follow us around, making everything seem less enjoyable and our lives unpleasant.

For many, the way we choose to deal with these times of anxiety and frustration only makes matters worse. We may even find that we look for ways to distract our minds from the present challenges so we can get through a tough situation at hand. Sometimes, we may choose to zone out in front of a television or to withdraw from the reality of our life in pursuit of some guilty pleasure. Some people have experienced such grievous circumstances and events in their life that no words can describe the pain and suffering that follows.

Many of us have chosen to cut loose on the weekends, attempting to forget the stress our life brought during the week. We may want to escape from the stress of a job that wears us down, from a bad relationship, or from a family situation that burdens us. We could turn to less than productive methods to get away from reality in search of a temporary reprieve. We may resort to unhealthy indulgences of bad food or irresponsible retail therapy to make ourselves feel better. Others may search for an escape through some form of substance abuse or high-risk activities.

I have been as guilty as anyone of trying to drown my woes on the weekend in an attempt to forget my troubles or life stressors. Others may find themselves at the edge of a cliff made up of anger, remorse, or regret that leaves the impression no solution exists that will repair the damage they have suffered. The one thing that is common with most coping strategies is the reality that pain, suffering and anxiety are still there to meet us after we attempt escape. Many times, our problems are only compounded by the consequences of attempted stress release. That consequence may be the debt racked up by retail therapy, the guilt and indigestion from over-indulging on junk food, or the headache left after a night of drinking. What each of these strategies has in common is that the result leaves us no better than we were before the action.

An act of charity may appear too simple to provide any kind of relief from our woes. But, to the contrary, giving of yourself to a cause greater than you can be very effective. When we take a moment to contribute to a charitable cause, the positive energy we create can provide momentary relief from our troubles. When you think about the troubles of another and act in some way to make things better, your mind is distracted from the problems you face in your own life. Besides, the physical changes that occur when you are oriented toward another literally mean that you are in a different brain state.

We have circuits in our brain called "mirror neurons" that are the hardware of empathy and connection. Some people have a mirror neuron system that is highly sensitive and responds empathically to almost any living thing. Others have a mirror neuron system that is less sensitive and responds only to similar people. Sometimes, as with psychopaths, these mirror neurons respond to no one. For the rest of us, our ability to bond with others is hard-wired into the brain.

Our capacity to relate with others goes beyond the conscious level; in some ways, we are programmed to be copycats. When we see another person performing an action, for example, the motor areas of our brains that would be activated if we were to do the same action, are stimulated. For example, if you were to see a person swinging a golf club, the same motor areas of the brain involved in swinging a golf club are also activated in your brain, even though you are not conscious of this. This level of identification not only enables you to feel empathy, but also understand what is going on in their heads. This is the so-called "theory of mind" which drives a lot of our social behavior.

The mirror neuron system and theory of mind are what move people to take action when they see someone in distress. Without these mechanisms, charities could show as many photos as they wished of starving and deprived children, but they would get little to no response. The brain, therefore, is wired for empathy and compassion.

Will an act of charity make everything we have experienced in the past go away? No. Will a generous contribution to a worthy cause undo a tragedy we have had to endure? No. Will our woes of yesterday still exist tomorrow if we give of ourselves unselfishly? Yes, they probably will. But will an act of charity, a time of thinking of someone else, a moment of giving of ourselves to someone in a much worse situation make our own burden a little easier to bear? You would be surprised at how effective it might be.

Can every act of charity give us a little positive energy, a momentary reprieve, a good feeling to enjoy in our hearts?

Absolutely. Most significantly, an act of charity won't compound our situation or make matters worse than they already are. When we wake up the next day, we might still have some residual pain and anguish to deal with, but things will be a little brighter. We might have a different perspective.

One act of kindness or contribution to a cause may not be enough to undo the struggles you face in your own life, but it will make those struggles a little easier. If your heart aches from the loss of a loved one, maybe a perpetual effort will help you through the pain. It may take weeks or months of focusing on another, greater cause, but through charity, you can find the way.

I have a good friend, Brian Cardoza, who experienced a more horrific childhood than anyone should ever know. Many like him have sacrificed their lives in the pursuit of substances that will numb their pain. In order to combat his own demons, Brian founded an organization known as The Broken Knee Club[2], devoted to helping others who are survivors of sexual, physical or mental abuse.

Brian has devoted a significant portion of his time and energy to helping others in need, specifically those who have experienced the horrors he has known. This has been the solution to his own suffering. Serving a charitable effort by helping others in need has provided greater comfort and reprieve from

---

2 To find out more about the Broken Knee Club, visit http://www.brokenkneeclub. org/

his own suffering than any artificial substance or risky behavior could have provided.

Whether the challenges you presently face are minor and temporary or severe and long lasting, you will experience a positive result through the kind act of giving to charity or helping another in need. The next time you face frustration or angst in your life, take a moment to contribute to a charity or perform an act of kindness for another. Then reflect on the good that you have done. Many things in life that happen to us, we cannot control. Some frustrations are unavoidable. One thing we can control is the contribution we make to another and the positive feeling we get as a result.

» ACTION

> WHEN FACING A STRESSOR in your life, take a momentary reprieve from the anguish and stop and make a charitable donation and/or commit an act in kindness. The greater your anguish, the more acts you should commit.

CHAPTER SIX

What Goes Around, Comes Around

"Serve the world unselfishly and profit."
–Ezra Firestone

HAVE YOU EVER wondered what people mean by "good karma" or wondered what might be a cause for a streak of good luck?

I once heard a very enlightening philosophy on charitable giving by Ezra Firestone (www.smartmarketer.com). Ezra explained the connection between charity, the Universe and the cause for things like luck, good fortune and karma. His philosophy about charity suggests when we give to charity or commit a selfless act for another, we have created a debt of goodwill with the Universe. Our selfless acts toward another create positive energy in the world, making the world just a little better for all. This contribution of positive energy creates future goodwill that will someday be repaid to us. We may never make the connection between a good deed we commit and the repayment, because the two events are seldom related. However, what we might only see as a stroke of good luck or a result of good karma may actually be the Universe repaying a previous good deed or act of charity.

Think of your acts of charity or goodwill as a deposit into a savings account with the Universe. The balance of goodwill you create will be repaid to you in some way in the future.

Giving to charity and committing selfless acts for another is, of course, the right thing to do. We often feel good inside as soon as the act is completed, but the benefit we gain goes much further. Create a debt of goodwill with the Universe, and you will be repaid this investment in the future. Control the "luck" that will come your way tomorrow by donating to a charity or helping a friend in need today.

There is one warning that comes with this advice that you should follow if you wish to maximize the benefit you receive from the Universe. If you publicize the work you do for charity or the contribution you have made, you will receive positive attention from those you share this with. The favorable impression you make may inspire people to act more kindly to you. This attention you get from others can be considered a partial payment from the Universe for your debt of goodwill.

If you feel the need to share the news of your charitable acts with others for the recognition and favor you may gain, you have already received your payment of goodwill.

To be most effective, to receive the greatest return from the Universe for your actions, give anonymously. When you boast about or collect recognition for your charitable contributions, you're collecting on the debt owed to you through the positive recognition you experience. It may not be "paid in full" when you accept recognition; but if you'd rather your debt of good be paid to you with success and future joy in your life, then make your contributions anonymously.

I do much of my charitable giving anonymously. Of course, I'm keeping records for my taxes, but I'm not boasting about it to the I.R.S or anyone else unnecessarily!

» ACTION

MAKE A CHARITABLE DONATION but be sure not to tell anyone about it. Or commit a few selfless acts of kindness for the benefit of another but hide your involvement in the act.

CHAPTER SEVEN
Make a Difference One Step at a Time

"If you can't feed a hundred people, then feed just one."
–Mother Teresa

STATISTICS ABOUT THE amount of need there is in this world are staggering. The magnitude of many of the global problems we face can be a hurdle that prevents people from getting involved. For example, recent figures suggest there are as many as one billion people on the planet that do not have access to clean drinking water. Poor nutrition and hunger are implicated in half of the 7.6 million deaths of children under five each year. In America alone, there are nearly 16,000 new cases and almost 2,000 deaths each year of kids suffering from cancer.

The amount of time and money that it would require to eradicate the world of the troubles we face is an investment so large no one can estimate it. The task of just solving one of these problems on a global scale may seem daunting, or even hopeless. I have thought to myself at times, "If there are four million kids in this world that are dying from hunger, what real difference will my little contribution to a food bank make?"

Is it even worth the effort when the numbers make a cause appear hopeless?

This, of course, is a terrible way to feel about charity or the act of making a contribution, but it is natural to have similar concerns when we face such a challenging feat. I once heard a story that has completely changed my beliefs about how my contribution, of any amount, can make a difference. When I relate this idea to others, I often refer to it as "The Starfish Theory":

One morning a father and son were walking down the beach. There had been a large storm the night before, so the beach was littered with starfish that had washed ashore. As the two walked along, the father kept bending down to pick up starfish and chucking them back in the ocean.

After a couple of minutes, the young boy finally asked, "Dad, why are you throwing the starfish back in the water?"

"Son, this starfish needs to be back in the ocean to survive. Every starfish I pick up and throw back will not die."

"Dad, there are thousands of starfish littered up and down the beach; what possible difference could it make if you throw back a few?"

The father paused for a moment before he knelt down to pick up another. With one starfish in his hand, he looked at his son and said, "Son, for this starfish in my hand, it makes all the difference in the world."

It only takes about $30 to provide water for a man, woman or child in need[3]. UNICEF reports that just $1.50 is enough to provide a child with a life-saving vaccine[4]. The Feeding America Organization can provide as many as ten meals to a starving child in America with a $10 donation.

Does helping one child or saving one life go far to eradicate all the hunger, pain or suffering in the world? No, not even close. But for the few people you can personally affect with your donation, for the couple of lives you can save, for the family and loved ones of those people in need; your small donation **can make all the difference in the world.**

You don't have to wait until you can afford to make a massive contribution to a charity to get started. You don't need to give $1,000 or even $100 to start making a difference. Give what you can, when you can, and you will still help to make

3 http://www.charitywater.org/whywater/ (Nov 19, 2014)
4 http://www.cdc.gov/vaccines/programs/vfc/awardees/vaccine-management/price-list/index.html (Nov 19, 2014)

a difference in the world. Every little bit helps, and just a little can make a difference.

» ACTION

OVER THE NEXT WEEK, take a moment to make a small contribution to at least five charities. Just a few dollars to the right cause will make all the difference in the world.

CHAPTER EIGHT
Your Own Passion

"It is the ultimate luxury to combine passion and contribution. It's also a very clear path to happiness."
–Sheryl Sandberg

BELIEVE EVERY DONATION of time, energy or money that someone gives to help a cause is a noble gesture. Many organizations are doing fantastic work to make the world a better place or to improve the lives of those in need. A contribution to any such cause is a great thing.

To experience the greatest benefit from your charitable contributions and acts of generosity, find a cause that resonates with you. There are many causes that one can support; some may appeal to you more than others. We all have personal experiences or beliefs that make us feel one specific cause is more important than others are. Focus your time and energy toward making a difference with that cause and your effort will create the most positive effect for you.

When you support a cause that you believe in, it will be easier to sustain your support and make the sacrifice of time and energy required. When I give to a charity that supports the cause that resonates with me the most, I feel the greatest benefit of positive energy and feeling of achievement.

I am passionate about helping to bring water to all those who lack access to it. A dear friend of mine, Brandon Gillotti, made me aware of an enormous opportunity to help. Brandon had done some work raising money and awareness for an organization that made urban filtration systems. I was intrigued by what I learned about this cause, so I began to make small donations to help. When I learned more about the nature of the water problem around the world, the need resonated with me so much that it became a life passion to contribute. Here is what I have written on my fundraising website about this cause and why I am vested in making a difference with this need:

> *My Passion: charity: water reports that more than 748 million people who do not have access to clean drinking water; some estimate that number to be closer to one billion.*

> *Many of us have no idea what it's like to be thirsty. We have plenty of water to drink – even the water in our toilets is clean!*

But many people around the world don't have that luxury. Every day, 5,000 kids die from water-related illnesses before they reach their fifth birthday. But it doesn't have to be that way. There are simple solutions like drilled wells, spring protections and BioSand filters that help provide clean water to communities around the world.

It has become a passion of mine to spread awareness and raise money to make a difference with water. I applaud every effort to help combat disease in developing countries or to provide food for the millions of starving people. But water is a human's most basic need. A person can live a few minutes without air. The next most crucial resource for survival is water; without it, a person cannot survive more than a few days.

Without water, a person doesn't think about hunger. Without water, thirst will take a person's life before any disease. Without water, people cannot take care of themselves, much less care for others. When people don't have access to clean drinking water, they cannot begin to work on building communities, starting businesses to support themselves or educating their children. Without water, there is nothing but poverty and the threat of terror every single day.

Millions of woman and children spend hours each day walking to collect water for their family. Often, the only water they can find is muddy or contaminated with life- threatening bacteria. The hours spent collecting water rob children of an opportunity to gain an education. The time spent collecting water prevents women from earning money for their families or contributing to commerce in their communities.

To me, this water crisis is the direst need we can address. When I make a contribution to the world's water crisis, it makes me feel the greatest benefit from my charitable contributions. If you have one cause that resonates with you the most, then focus your time and effort on helping with that cause. You don't have to give to every cause you see in order to make a difference in the world; do what makes you feel the best and make a difference where you are inspired to do so.

» ACTION

SPEND A FEW MINUTES thinking about the world's greatest troubles. Make a list of one to five causes that pain you the most to think about. If there is just one cause that stands out from the rest, circle it and reflect on what you might do to help.

CHAPTER NINE
Quick and Easy Giving

"For it is in giving that we receive."
–St. Francis of Assisi

MAKING A DONATION to a charity doesn't have to be challenging or time consuming. You don't have to wait for the next solicitation to come in the mail or for someone to come knocking on the door to find a charity to give to.

Some people may be concerned about making online donations to charity for fear they are vulnerable by giving out credit card information on the internet. It doesn't take much to create a website and collect donations. Millions of organizations are claiming to make a difference. How can you tell which groups are doing the work they claim and are actually making a difference?

Fortunately, there are some fantastic companies with reputable organizations and established websites making it very easy to give to almost any charity at any time. If you already know what charitable cause you would like to contribute to, chances are they have a website set up to collect donations online. A quick Google search will direct you to a website for well-established organizations that support many noble causes. If you are unsure whom you would like to donate to or what organizations are providing help to a specific cause, there are many online databases that can help.

One website that may help you in making donations is justgive.org. JustGive has a database of more than 1.8 million charitable organizations working throughout the world. Each organization that is in the site's database has been registered with the IRS, and the charity information listed is provided through GuideStare®. You can do a very quick search on Just-Give to find organizations by cause, location or name.

Two other sites I have used myself are http://charitynavigator.org and http://greatnonprofits.org. While you cannot donate to organizations through these sites as you can with www.justgive.org, they can be great research tools. Each offers ratings and reviews for the various charities in their database so you can learn what the organization has done in the past and will do with your donation.

Once you find a charity that interests you, justgive.org makes it very easy to make a secure online contribution to the charity you chose. You can make a one-time contribution or set up recurring donations. The site is user friendly, secure and easy to use. You can set up a quick user account that will track your donations, create a list of your favorite causes and, if you choose, will save your credit card information to make future giving fast and easy. One great feature of justgive.org that was a benefit for me last year: you can print a year-end summary of all the donations you have made. This saves you from having to compile records for every donation throughout the year.

We have discussed many of the personal benefits you can experience when giving to charity. The great feeling you have and the positive energy you create in your day make a big difference. I once had a very upsetting and bleak period in my life not long ago. Determined to take control of my emotional state and make the best of the difficult period, I decided to focus my energy outward and try to do something positive.

One step I took to take control of my energy and mood was to experiment with giving to charity every day for a month. It became sort of a ritual to make a small donation to a charity each morning. Instead of allowing my current struggle to affect my emotions and manifest negative energy in my life, I started each day by making a small donation to a variety of different charities throughout the month. Like a multivitamin for my soul, I ensured that my day started on a positive note by doing something for someone else.

The effect this experiment had was greater than anything

I could have expected. For a small donation of $10 made through justgive.org each morning, I experienced a wonder you wouldn't understand if you hadn't tried it for yourself. The $300 I invested over the month was worth every penny for the effect it had on my mood and outlook on life.

This is a great experiment to do at any time in your life, but if you are experiencing a particularly difficult situation, I cannot recommend highly enough that you give this experiment a try. You may not have the money right now to make a $10 donation every day, but that doesn't have to stop you. I chose to make a monetary donation, but as we discussed previously, there are many kinds of charitable contributions you can make. The contribution does not need to be for a charity; any act of kindness you commit for another will create the same effect. You could do a favor for a neighbor or help a friend. You could send a pleasant note to a person who would appreciate it or deliver an unexpected yet sincere compliment to someone you pass by. Anything that creates a positive balance of goodwill in the Universe.

The feeling it will give you is worth every ounce of effort. The positive energy you feel will help carry you through a difficult time. It's true, a small donation or kind gesture won't undo a breakup, get your job back, or bring back a loved one who recently passed, but a small gesture will lend you a moment of reprieve from your suffering and help you through the day a little easier. Positive energy grows no matter the donation size and no matter what challenge you are confronting.

Don't think you need to wait until you hit a rough patch to give this experiment a try. If things are going well in your life and you feel particularly blessed, see how far you can take that joy in the positive direction. Wouldn't we all like to enjoy a little more happiness, experience a little more abundance or feel more blessed?

» ACTION

Set aside some time to spend at least twenty to thirty minutes exploring the charities listed on justgive.org, charitynavigator.org or any other web resources. If you have a particular cause from the last action step that resonates with you the most, search for organizations that focus on that cause.

CHAPTER TEN

The Next Level

*"Many small people in small places doing
small things can change the world."*
–Eduardo Galeano

SOON AFTER I became passionately involved with the opportunity to provide water to those in need, I made it a personal mission to spread awareness and inspire others to contribute to the cause. I was happy with the money I had been able to donate and the time I was able to give, but I wanted to compound my efforts by inspiring more people to help.

Supporting a cause that you find most important may inspire you to take your charitable contribution to the next level. J.P. Getty said he would rather gain 1% support from 100 people than to get 100% from 1 person. That quote may not make sense at first. Wouldn't the two sides of that equation both add to 100%? Well, not exactly. If you gave 100% of yourself toward a cause, it would require you to sacrifice everything else in your life and there would only be so much work you could complete. You would have no time for rest, for planning or for taking care of yourself. Most of us must do something to support ourselves and earn a living. If you gave 100% of yourself to a single cause, you probably wouldn't be able to sustain that effort for very long before running out of money or facing exhaustion.

If, on the other hand, you were able to inspire the help of 100 people to give 1% of what they had to give, you would have a sustainable effort that contributed that same 100% – at least in the beginning. What happens when those 100 people give 1% and then share their experience with others? When 100 people help, you spread the word and attract more contributors. The difference you are able to make grows exponentially.

So, spreading awareness is part of charity, too. If you currently don't have any money to donate, inspiring others to donate can be a great option. Fortunately, there are some great aids out there to help in just this venture. For example, justgive.org also provides the ability to easily create a personal campaign page. With justgive.org, and multiple other charity activism platforms, you can develop a campaign to raise money and awareness for nearly any cause.

In just a few minutes, you can launch a personal webpage to promote your cause and collect donations. If you want to maximize the difference you can make, devote some of your charitable time and energy to spreading awareness and inspiring others to contribute. It doesn't take much work to launch you own campaign. Companies like charitywater.org and just-give.org have done all the hard work for you.

MY PERSONAL EXPERIENCE

If you wish to take your personal contributions to the next level, I have found it best to take the time to inspire others to join you in that cause. Spread awareness about the particular need you are supporting and educate others about the cause you believe in.

I first took my charitable involvement to the next level in May of 2014 when I launched my first charity: water campaign. charity: water, like many other organizations, has made it extremely easy to get involved and start a personal campaign[5]. With a few clicks of a mouse and a short blurb about your inspiration, you can start a campaign, set a fundraising goal and begin inviting friends, family members and complete strangers to your campaign page. Once your page is up and running, driving traffic to it is easy with an occasional Tweet, Facebook post, email or quick plug on any other social media

---

5 Two platforms I have used personally for personal campaigns are justgive.org and charitywater.org. For information on setting up you own campaign, visit: https://www.justgive.org/registries or https://my.charitywater.org/p/campaignCreate

platform you prefer. I chose to also make some easy and inexpensive flyers to market my campaign and hung them at the coffee shops and retail stores in town.

If you are interested, I would recommend having some inexpensive business cards printed to help promote your page. As you get involved with your own campaign, you will certainly become excited about it and begin mentioning it to almost everyone you meet. It is easy to share your excitement and intrigue someone to get involved, but you need to make sure they remember your campaign and website the next time they are by a computer and have a credit card in hand. I decided to create a small business-card-sized reminder that would give people the information they needed for later. Something they would pull out of their pocket at the end of the day. Maybe even lay it on a counter or nightstand where it would be a constant reminder until they made a donation.

You can make some cards to try out for yourself. They now sell very nice, non-perforated, business cards you can use in your home printer to make as few as 10 cards at a time. You can buy these Avery cards online or at your local office supply store. I used VistaPrint and created a very simple card that said nothing more than "Make a Difference" with a picture of a water jug and the web address of my campaign page.

The result – in just over 90 days I sent a dozen emails, posted to Facebook about 20 times and passed out 100 cards. I inspired 61 others to join my cause and help my campaign; together we raised $7,133 in support. I only share my experience and the success of my first campaign to demonstrate how easy it can be. This isn't an exhaustive training about hosting a campaign, but it should give you a few ideas to get you started.

If you have participated in a charity before or made a personal contribution, you understand the good feeling doing so creates. If you think that is good, wait until you experience how great it feels to inspire 25 to 50 others to join your cause. When you reach out for help from others, there is no limit to how far you can go or how much of a difference you can inspire. Sometimes, your action alone is enough to get the ball rolling on a combined effort that far surpasses what you might have ever imagined. The story behind the founders of charity: water illustrates that example perfectly.

charity: water is an amazing organization that has epitomized the effect of taking a charitable contribution to the next level. charity: water began in 2006 when founder Steve Harrison invited a few friends together to help support his cause. By the end of 2013, charity: water had raised more than $100 million dollars! This money has been used to provide clean drinking water to an estimated 4.4 million people across 22 developing countries. The tremendous results that charity: water has achieved by taking their involvement to the next level is a perfect example of how much difference a few people can make when they leverage the help of others.

There are many other wonderful companies that are doing similarly amazing things with charity. Maybe there is one that you can become involved with that is addressing a need you are passionate about. You can find a few organizations that you might care to become involved with by using the web resources mentioned in this book.

MY PERSONAL APPEAL

It is a personal mission of mine to get involved and to help make a positive difference with the world's lack of clean drinking water. I have made an ambitious personal goal to help bring water to one million people during my lifetime. I plan to devote the majority of my charitable donations of time, money and energy to this goal. But, to achieve it, I will need the help of many others. I chose to take my charitable activities to the next level.

Just as the journey of a thousand miles begins with one step, the journey to bring water to one million people begins with the first dollar donated and the first campaign launched. To begin this journey, I requested the support of others to help spread the word and multiply the difference I could make. Please join me at www.onemilliongoal.org.

» ACTION

> STEP OUT OF YOUR COMFORT ZONE for a moment and share your passion with friends and family. Contact your network and tell them about your involvement in your charity. If you want to take it to the next level, encourage them to join you in your mission.

CHAPTER ELEVEN
The Best Way to Give

"No one has ever become poor by giving."
–Anne Frank

THE BEST CHARITY to give to, or the best cause to support, is a personal decision that depends on what resonates with each person. Similarly, the best way to give, or to get involved in a charity, works in the same way. Whatever way feels best to you or brings you the greatest feeling of contribution and accomplishment is the best way for you to give or become involved. I'm sharing my experiences and preferences, but how you choose to give should be determined by what feels the best to you.

First, you must decide how you will become involved in charity. Will you donate some time helping a local charity or will you spend your time and energy spreading awareness about a cause that you support? Maybe your act of charity won't involve a specific cause or organization at all.

If you chose not to make a monetary donation or devote your time to a charity, that doesn't mean you can't benefit from some of these many gifts. Maybe you are at a point in your life where no charitable cause resonates with you. You can still receive many of the gifts of giving through your acts of kindness toward others. Doing a favor for a friend or helping a loved one in need can create as much positive energy in the Universe and in the lives of the donor and recipient as a donation to charity. Even a gesture as simple as a thoughtful card or shared words of encouragement will make a difference to the recipient - and to you.

If you decide that making a monetary contribution to a charity is the best way for you to become involved, don't feel that you need to make a significant contribution to affect a significant difference in the world or in your own life. With a charitable contribution, like any meaningful or heartfelt gift, it is the thought that counts most.

Just as the starfish story illustrates, you don't need to make a massive contribution to a major cause in order to make a difference; just a few dollars can make all the difference in the world for one life affected by your good will. When a young child takes all his hard-earned couple of dollars from his piggy bank to purchase a thoughtful gift for a parent or sibling, there is an enormous emotional significance in that loving gesture. If a wealthy investor throws a few hundred dollars on an impulse gift with no meaning behind it, the significance pales in comparison to the loving gesture of the child. The difference – it's the thought that counts.

When you have a lot, give a lot. When you have a little, give a little. The importance is that you give, and give with meaning and compassion.

An effective way to make your charitable giving much easier is to automate the allocation of a portion of your income for charity. I have experienced, as I am sure you have, that it is very hard to reach into your pocket and make a significant contribution to a charity when that money is competing with your other financial obligations.

I used to run my personal finances by receiving a paycheck and then paying all of my bills. Like many of us, I would then spend the rest of my money on the more discretionary uses of my income like groceries, entertainment and desired purchases. I once included charity in this category of discretionary spending. My charitable donations came from the money that was left in my checking account or in my pocket after my bills were paid.

The major problem with this arrangement is the conflict between my desire for donating to charity and my desire for paying for other expenses, like purchasing things for myself or enjoying my time off by going to dinner or buying tickets for a concert. It is a greater stretch to give generously to a charitable cause when the donation conflicts with your other wants. Even when it doesn't actually steal food from your mouth by costing you grocery money, it may feel like it if faced with a compulsive decision between giving and enjoying your hard earned money.

The better approach, which I now use, is to allocate a certain amount of my paycheck for charitable giving. I now have an allotment pulled directly from my paycheck that goes into a separate account for future charitable donations. I am no longer used to the money being in my checking account or in my hot little hands, so it doesn't feel like I am sacrificing unduly to support a charitable cause. The money in my charity account is used solely for that purpose. If I have $50 left in my pocket at the end of the month but $250 in my charity account, it is no longer a conflict to give to a charity I am compassionate about.

The best way to give is the way that best fulfills its highest purpose. The purpose of giving is to create a positive energy for the donor and the beneficiary. Don't allow the potential for the act of charity to feed a negative emotion within. Let this wonderful act be the positive and joyful experience it should be, not one that creates conflict or heartache in a part of your mind.

When the act of giving conflicts directly with other wants and needs, the positive vibration you could create in your heart is tarnished by the fear that money donated may be needed for something else. If you pay your fuel bill, grocery bill and make charitable donations from the same pot, each obligation competes with the others. When your charitable involvement comes from an account set aside for that purpose, and you declare it will only be used for charity, no angst or remorse is attached to your donation.

There are many programs that make it very easy to donate to charity. Some even automate your donation for you each month. If you cannot set a normal schedule or don't feel that you can trust yourself with a savings account holding that charity money, then an automatic contribution may be an effective method for your monetary donation. If, however, you trust yourself to use the charity money for just that purpose, I highly advise against automatic charitable contributions.

This advice goes back to a point mentioned before – it is the thought that counts. When you automate your contribution, your charitable donation is out of sight, out of mind. You have the thought of the donation maybe twice, once when you take the action to set up the donation and again when you get your year-end statement or file your taxes. If you have that thought only twice a year, then you are only benefiting from this positive contribution to the world on those two occasions. You are still doing a great good for the people you affect with your donations, but you do not get to enjoy the full effect of your action.

Maybe you will remember often throughout the year that you are making a difference because you think of your automatic donation, but it won't be as significant an event as making regular decisive actions and donations throughout the year.

Imagine this scenario – What if you set up a service so that every anniversary or birthday, a gift is automatically mailed to your friend or loved one along with some auto-generated card? What emotional effect would that gift-giving create for you, or your recipient, if he or she knew it was automated? What if you had forgotten about the occasion until they called thanking you for the gift you sent? Would you feel the same warm emotion as if you had just spent hours picking the perfect gift and writing a thoughtful card? Remember, feelings beget actions, but actions also generate feelings.

If your charitable contributions come from your actions and not monetary donations, you can still benefit from these ideas. Automate the allocation of your time. Set a schedule and stick to it. I have a good friend who commits one Saturday morning a month to volunteering at a soup kitchen. He schedules his time at the soup kitchen first and then schedules the rest of his life around it. There is no conflict between his personal time and his charitable time because he schedules his soup kitchen involvement first.

Get the most enjoyment you can from your giving. That enjoyment comes when you take action and give the donation. When you feel the joy and gratitude in your own heart many times throughout the year, it inspires you to keep giving in the future. If you get no joy from the action, it is too easy for the habit to disappear. We spend money on what we enjoy the most. Giving to charity can be one of those things you get the most joy and happiness from if you do it in the right way. Remember, the gifts you receive come from the action, they come from the selfless gesture; it is the thought that counts. Have that thought more than once a year, have it every month, every week or every day if that is how you most enjoy giving.

» ACTION

ALLOCATE A CERTAIN AMOUNT of money from each paycheck for charity. Set that amount aside before you start spending the rest of it. If you want, set up a specific charity bank account or set aside a specific time of the week or month to give. If you wish to make a contribution by volunteering at a local organization, create an appointment on your calendar and stick to it.

CHAPTER TWELVE
The Winning Lotto Ticket

"No act of kindness, no matter
how small, is ever wasted."
–Aesop

THIS PARTING STORY about charity exemplifies one of the most important aspects about charity.

A few weeks before I decided to write this book, I enjoyed one of those interesting and rare life experiences that leave an indelible impression, one that will last for many years to come.

I was standing in line at a local convenience store one Saturday afternoon. Now, I couldn't tell you what I had for breakfast yesterday, but I have a vivid memory of this one afternoon. The gentleman in front of me in line seemed a very positive and happy person. He wasn't obnoxiously loud or unpleasant in any way; he just had a big smile on him and greeted everyone near with a friendly and energetic hello. There was no doubt this guy was having a wonderful afternoon and that his positive attitude was felt by all those nearby.

When this gentleman reached the front of the line, he placed his soda on the counter and asked for a few scratch-off tickets. He didn't take time to play the game on the cards; he just took a few seconds to scratch off the barcode that would reveal the numbers to be scanned by the machine. (If you have never had an opportunity to play a scratch-off, there is a large section of the card that one scratches off to play whatever matching game the card entails. At the bottom of the card, typically, there is a small area that reveals the special barcode or serial number that the computer reads to know if the card is a winner.)

He then handed the cards over to the cashier and asked if she would please scan them. With astonishment in her voice and a smile on her face, the cashier gladly announced this man had struck some luck and the first scratch-off was in fact a $25 winner. She scanned the second card; it too was a winner, this time $50! The gentleman was certainly pleased by the great return on his $10 investment. What struck me as odd; he didn't seem at all surprised by his good fortune. The cashier proceeded to ring this guy up for his soda and cash him out for the lotto winnings he had won.

After the transaction was complete and without hesitation, the guy folded up a twenty dollar bill from his winnings and handed it to the cashier with a smile. She tried to refuse the money but the guy left the money on the counter and turned for the door saying, "Have a wonderful rest of your weekend."

As he made it for the door, I commented aloud that the gesture of sharing his winnings was extremely generous and not something many people would do. He then turned to me and said, "If you don't share the blessings you receive with others, the Universe will stop sharing blessings with you."

Wow! What a simple but powerful message. A truth about life summed up in just a few words.

One point about this experience with the winning scratch-offs that really impressed me; this guy hadn't received a huge sum of money with this fortunate event. Yes, $75 would be nice to have, but I don't think he was contemplating retirement from it.

Many times, we make the excuse that we will share our fortune or make a contribution to charity once our ship comes in; once we stash a little more money away for our family, or we get that next raise. "Let me just take care of a few things I need to, and then I will be more generous with what I have," is a thought I have had on occasion and a sentiment I have heard many share before. This experience in the convenience store taught me a great lesson – when you have a little, share a little; in the future when you have a lot, share a lot.

No matter who you are or where you are in life, you have many blessings to be grateful for. If you are holding a device in your hands that enables you to read this book, if you are in relatively good health, have enjoyed some sort of meal today or had access to clean water, there are already things in your life that many people do not have the fortune to enjoy. You are blessed with many wonderful things that none of us should take for granted.

At times, I am just as guilty of forgetting my blessings as the next person. We all get caught up in the moment and in the challenges of life. Our mind wanders to the things that we wish we had, and we forget the many blessings we already enjoy. Charity provides a way to show our gratitude for the blessings we do have, to share the great fortune we enjoy in our own lives with those who are much less fortunate.

When we show gratitude and share our blessings with the world, no matter how small the contribution or the sacrifice, we open ourselves up to continue to receive the blessings we have. Just as the man explained to me that afternoon in the convenience store, if you want more good fortune and greater blessings to come your way in the future, share what you have today with others and the Universe will share more with you.

» ACTION

FOR THE NEXT WEEK, make an effort to go out of your way to be generous to the people you encounter. Keep a journal or write yourself an email to capture how the effort made you feel. If there is a particular time of day that is more stressful than others, make an effort to commit these acts during this time of day.

CONCLUSION

AN INTERESTING THING about the nature of giving is that when you give of yourself, you become more. The more you selflessly give, the more love, gratitude and fortune you experience in your own life. Jim Rohn says, "When somebody shares, everybody wins."

Bonding and helping others is hard-wired into our brains; we experience many benefits when we give. We have more energy, we reduce stress, we step outside our own egos and experience the world in a different way. We even become more spiritual.

Many of us know people who are truly happy. They enjoy an abundant lifestyle and generously share all they have with their friends and loved ones. We may often think of what we would do if we experienced great success or had a stroke of luck and won the lottery. We may talk about all the things we would buy for others or the donations we will make to charity once we have a lot to give. The fallacy of this approach is that giving brings you more to give. When you pour out of your cup of abundance, your cup grows so that you can experience more abundance in your own life.

When you are generous with what you have, the Universe becomes generous with what you receive. When you focus your energy on others, it makes your own woes easier to manage. When your mind is occupied with the stress in your own life, charity can ease that pain.

We could all enjoy a little more love, happiness and abundance in our lives. We can all use a little more good fortune and positive energy. We all have a tool that will pour a little more abundance into our own cup; charity is that tool.

Start today to make your tomorrow a little brighter. Take control and make the world a little better place to be; take better care of others and the Universe will take better care of you. Start today with building a better future for yourself and those in need. I truly hope you have gotten as much from this book as I have received from the life experiences I captured when writing it.

My involvement with charity has been an incredibly powerful joy that has brought many benefits to my life. For your future benefit, I have captured some of the most significant ideas from the text and put them in a quick reference for you below. If ever you find that you have forgotten these ideas, or if you find yourself facing a particularly troubling time in your life, refer to this list below and make your charitable actions a priority once again.

10-STEP ACTION CHECKLIST

1. RESEARCH www.justgive.org, http://greatnonprofits.org or www.charitynavigator.com to find a cause that inspires you.

2. START A JOURNAL of your charitable giving and acts of kindness.

3. WRITE DOWN a few causes that are especially meaningful to you.

4. REACH OUT to five people and express your appreciation of them. Take time to reflect on how you felt while doing that. What responses did you get back?

5. CREATE a special charity bank account or set aside a portion of your income to donate to a cause.

6. WHEN FEELING STRESSED, make a donation or commit an act of kindness toward another.

7. VOLUNTEER YOUR TIME in service to a friend or neighbor in need. Reflect on how it made you feel while you were doing it.

8. SPEND SOME TIME volunteering for people who are in need.

9. PROMOTE YOUR FAVORITE CHARITIES in some way – send a Tweet, make Facebook updates, send an email to friends, etc.

10. START A CAMPAIGN with an online charity platform. Inform your network about your pursuit and ask them to join your cause.

SPECIAL THANKS

THEY SAY IT takes a village to raise a child. I think something similar can be said about writing a book. This is not a long book by any means but I could not have produced it without the help of many others. More people have influenced the message of this book or helped with this its preparation than I could mention here.

Diane, thank you for scrubbing the many drafts and for the lessons in punctuation and grammar along the way.

Howard, thank you for your discussions about neurological responses. Your contributions to this book are invaluable.

ABOUT THE AUTHOR

IN ADDITION TO being a supporter of a few charitable organizations, Garret is a student of and advocate for the act of selfless giving in any of its forms. Garret's involvement with charity began with an occasional contribution to a local cause, a meager donation to a national organization, or tithing to his church. Garret, like many others, soon noticed that an interesting thing happened; the more he gave, and the more attention he gave to the act of charity, the more he received. Many benefits from the act of giving began to emerge, which brought new meaning and significance to the act. For everything he gave of himself, he received back positive energy and goodwill. The more often he gave, the more joy came from the act.

Garret recently founded his own charitable organization, One Million Goal, Inc. This organization promotes and will track the progress of Garret's personal life mission to raise enough money and awareness to help bring clean water to one million of the men, women and children in need. You can find out more about this organization and follow Garret's progress towards this lofty goal at www.onemilliongoal.org.

WOULD YOU LIKE TO USE THIS
BOOK FOR FUNDRAISING?

COPIES OF *CHARITY: THE GIFTS OF GIVING* are being made available at cost to sell as a fundraiser for your cause. When preparing for your next charitable event, consider offering this book in gratitude for a donation, as an inspiration to increase your involvement, or as motivation for your board to intensify their commitment.

Please email Garret Biss at garret@onemilliongoal.org for more information.